P9-CQL-984

Awesome KNOCK KNOCK JOKES for Kids

BOB PHILLIPS

HARVEST HOUSE PUBLISHERS

EUGENE, OREGON

Cover by Terry Dugan Design, Minneapolis, Minnesota

AWESOME KNOCK-KNOCK JOKES FOR KIDS
Copyright © 2006 by Bob Phillips
Published by Harvest House Publishers
Eugene, Oregon 97402

ISBN-13: 978-0-7369-1714-8
ISBN-10: 0-7369-1714-4
Product # 6917144

Printed in the United States of America

06 07 08 09 10 11 12 13 14 / BC-CF / 10 9 8 7 6 5 4 3 2

Contents

Knock, Knock! 5

The Door Is Closed! 10

Stop That Knocking! 15

Who's Hammering on the Door? 20

Open the Door! 25

Who's Pounding at the Door? 30

Let Me In! 35

Stop That Noise! 40

What's That Noise? 45

I'm All Knocked Out! 50

Knock It Off! 55

Who's Beating the Door Down? 60

Hold Your Horses! 65

Tap, Tap, Tap! 70

Stop Beating the Door! 75

What's That Rapping Noise? 80

The Doorbell Is Broken! 85

Please Go Away! 90

Stop That Pounding! 95

You Have the Wrong Address! 100

Who Is It? 105

Knock, Knock!

Knock, knock.
Who's there?
Abbe.
Abbe who?
Abbe stung me on the neck.

○ ○ ○

Knock, knock.
Who's there?
Alby.
Alby who?
Alby back in about an hour.

○ ○ ○

Knock, knock.
Who's there?
Abby.
Abby who?
Abby seeing you inside if you would open the door.

○ ○ ○

Knock, knock.
Who's there?
Ach.
Ach who?
Gesundheit! Do you have a cold?

○ ○ ○

Knock, knock.
Who's there?
Acid.
Acid who?

Acid I'll keep knocking until you're tired of hearing me knock-knock.

○ ○ ○

Knock, knock.
Who's there?
Adam.
Adam who?
Adam up, $2 + 2 = 4$.

○ ○ ○

Knock, knock.
Who's there?
Agatha.
Agatha who?
Agatha awful tired of knocking and knocking.

○ ○ ○

Knock, knock.
Who's there?
Fletcher.
Fletcher who?
Fletcher hand open the door.

○ ○ ○

Knock, knock.
Who's there?
A herd.
A herd who?
A herd you like knock-knock jokes.

○ ○ ○

Knock, knock.
Who's there?
Aida.

Aida who?
Aida big pizza and now I'm full.

○ ○ ○

Knock, knock.
Who's there?
Aisle.
Aisle who?
Aisle be seeing you in all the old familiar places.

○ ○ ○

Knock, knock.
Who's there?
Alaska.
Alaska who?
Alaska all my friends why you're not opening the door.

○ ○ ○

Knock, knock.
Who's there?
Albee.
Albee who?
Albee seeing you later.

○ ○ ○

Knock, knock.
Who's there?
Alby.
Alby who?
Alby glad when you finally open the door.

○ ○ ○

Knock, knock.
Who's there?
Ida.

Ida who?
Ida rather be inside; it's cold out here.

○ ○ ○

Knock, knock.
Who's there?
Alex.
Alex who?
Alex chocolate chip cookies.

○ ○ ○

Knock, knock.
Who's there?
House.
House who?
House about letting me in, silly?

○ ○ ○

Knock, knock.
Who's there?
Ali.
Ali who?
Ali want to do is come inside.

○ ○ ○

Knock, knock.
Who's there?
Annie.
Annie who?
Annie one home?

○ ○ ○

Knock, knock.
Who's there?
Alma.

Alma who?
Alma getting tired of waiting for you to open the door.

○ ○ ○

Knock, knock.
Who's there?
Almond.
Almond who?
Almond love watching football games.

○ ○ ○

Knock, knock.
Who's there?
Alpaca.
Alpaca who?
Alpaca my bags and leave if you don't let me in.

○ ○ ○

Knock, knock.
Who's there?
Alpha.
Alpha who?
Alpha crying out loud, please open the door!

The Door Is Closed!

Knock, knock.
Who's there?
Amahl.
Amahl who?
Amahl is where I like to go shopping.

○ ○ ○

Knock, knock.
Who's there?
A Mayan.
A Mayan who?
A Mayan the wrong block, knocking on the wrong door?

○ ○ ○

Knock, knock.
Who's there?
Amish.
Amish who?
Amish you a whole lot.

○ ○ ○

Knock, knock.
Who's there?
Amoeba.
Amoeba who?
Amoeba silly, but I like knock-knock jokes.

○ ○ ○

Knock, knock.
Who's there?
Amos.
Amos who?
Amos be bugging you a lot.

○ ○ ○

Knock, knock.
Who's there?
Ancient.
Ancient who?
Ancient going to let me in?

○ ○ ○

Knock, knock.
Who's there?
Andy.
Andy who?
Andy pandy puddin' and pie…kissed the girls and made them cry.

○ ○ ○

Knock, knock.
Who's there?
Anita.
Anita who?
Anita someone to open the door.

○ ○ ○

Knock, knock.
Who's there?
Anna.
Anna who?
Anna one, Anna two, Anna three.

○ ○ ○

Knock, knock.
Who's there?
Annapolis.
Annapolis who?

Annapolis something I eat every day to keep the doctor away.

○ ○ ○

Knock, knock.
Who's there?
Annapolis.
Annapolis who?
Annapolis what Adam and Eve ate.

○ ○ ○

Knock, knock.
Who's there?
Lettuce.
Lettuce who?
Lettuce in. We brought the salad with us.

○ ○ ○

Knock, knock.
Who's there?
Snow.
Snow who?
Snow body likes knock-knock jokes like me.

○ ○ ○

Knock, knock.
Who's there?
Area.
Area who?
Area deaf? Can't you hear me knocking?

○ ○ ○

Knock, knock.
Who's there?
Argo.

Argo who?
Argo knock on someone else's door…they'll let me in.

O O O

Knock, knock.
Who's there?
Aria.
Aria who?
Aria tired of hearing knock-knock jokes?

O O O

Knock, knock.
Who's there?
Armageddon.
Armageddon who?
Armageddon out of here as fast as I can.

O O O

Knock, knock.
Who's there?
Dog Barry.
Dog Barry who?
Dog Barry his bone in the backyard.

O O O

Knock, knock.
Who's there?
Olive.
Olive who?
Olive to hear new knock-knock jokes.

O O O

Knock, knock.
Who's there?
Asia.

Asia who?
Asia finally going to open the door?

o o o

Knock, knock.
Who's there?
Wanda.
Wanda who?
Wanda hold my hand?

o o o

Knock, knock.
Who's there?
Atom.
Atom who?
Atom bomb. That joke blew up.

o o o

Knock, knock.
Who's there?
Augusta.
Augusta who?
Augusta wind can turn into a tornado.

Stop That Knocking!

Knock, knock.
Who's there?
Auto.
Auto who?
Auto open the door.

○ ○ ○

Knock, knock.
Who's there?
Yoda.
Yoda who?
Yoda funniest person I've ever seen.

○ ○ ○

Knock, knock.
Who's there?
Avenue.
Avenue who?
Avenue heard me knocking?

○ ○ ○

Knock, knock.
Who's there?
Avenue.
Avenue who?
Avenue gotten tired of all these knock-knock jokes?

○ ○ ○

Knock, knock.
Who's there?
Aware.
Aware who?
Aware, aware has my little dog gone?

○ ○ ○

Knock, knock.
Who's there?
Axe.
Axe who?
Axe me to tell another knock-knock joke.

○ ○ ○

Knock, knock.
Who's there?
Kenya.
Kenya who?
Kenya open the door? It's cold and I'm hungry.

○ ○ ○

Knock, knock.
Who's there?
Bach.
Bach who?
Bach door is locked also.

○ ○ ○

Knock, knock.
Who's there?
Barbie.
Barbie who?
Barbie-cue hot dogs are my favorite.

○ ○ ○

Knock, knock.
Who's there?
Barry.
Barry who?
Barry funny knock-knock jokes, aren't they?

○ ○ ○

Knock, knock.
Who's there?
Barton.
Barton who?
Barton down your coat; it's snowing.

○ ○ ○

Knock, knock.
Who's there?
Bat.
Bat who?
Bat you don't know, do you?

○ ○ ○

Knock, knock.
Who's there?
Bay.
Bay who?
Bay-be I'll tell you if you open the door.

○ ○ ○

Knock, knock.
Who's there?
Bayou.
Bayou who?
Bayou an ice cream cone if you let me in.

○ ○ ○

Knock, knock.
Who's there?
Bea.
Bea who?
Bea kind to me and open the door.

○ ○ ○

Knock, knock.
Who's there?
Shore.
Shore who?
Shore glad you like knock-knock jokes.

○ ○ ○

Knock, knock.
Who's there?
Beans.
Beans who?
Beans a long time waiting for you to open the door.

○ ○ ○

Knock, knock.
Who's there?
Bear.
Bear who?
Bear, oh bear has my little sheep gone?

○ ○ ○

Knock, knock.
Who's there?
Beater.
Beater who?
Beater beater pumpkin eater had a wife and couldn't feed her.

○ ○ ○

Knock, knock.
Who's there?
Ben.
Ben who?
Ben knocking forever out here.

○ ○ ○

Knock, knock.
Who's there?
Betty.
Betty who?
Betty gets sore knuckles from all that knocking.

○ ○ ○

Knock, knock.
Who's there?
Black Panther.
Black Panther who?
Black Panther all I have to wear.

○ ○ ○

Knock, knock.
Who's there?
Boo.
Boo who?
Stop it, you don't have to cry about it.

Who's Hammering on the Door?

Knock, knock.
Who's there?
Board.
Board who?
Board to death.

o o o

Knock, knock.
Who's there?
Boycott.
Boycott who?
Boycott is what little boys sleep on.

o o o

Knock, knock.
Who's there?
Boyd.
Boyd who?
Boyd, do I wish you'd stop telling knock-knock jokes.

o o o

Knock, knock.
Who's there?
Brighton.
Brighton who?
Brighton early the sun will come up.

o o o

Knock, knock.
Who's there?
Buster.

Buster who?
Buster gut if you laugh too hard.

○ ○ ○

Knock, knock.
Who's there?
Butter.
Butter who?
Butter open the door.

○ ○ ○

Knock, knock.
Who's there?
Butternut.
Butternut who?
Butternut come outside; it's raining.

○ ○ ○

Knock, knock.
Who's there?
Bwana.
Bwana who?
Bwana hear a good knock-knock joke?

○ ○ ○

Knock, knock.
Who's there?
Calcutta.
Calcutta who?
Calcutta hole in my pants.

○ ○ ○

Knock, knock.
Who's there?
Camphor.

Camphor who?
Camphor the life of me remember your name.

○ ○ ○

Knock, knock.
Who's there?
Candice.
Candice who?
Candice be the last time you tell me these crazy knock-knock jokes?

○ ○ ○

Knock, knock.
Who's there?
Candidate.
Candidate who?
Candidate for the birthday party be changed?

○ ○ ○

Knock, knock.
Who's there?
Cargo.
Cargo who?
Cargo, "Beep, beep!"

○ ○ ○

Knock, knock.
Who's there?
Carmen.
Carmen who?
Carmen down the road at full speed!

○ ○ ○

Knock, knock.
Who's there?

Carrie.
Carrie who?
Carrie me; I'm tired of walking.

o o o

Knock, knock.
Who's there?
Cashew.
Cashew who?
Cashew stealing candy and you'll go to jail.

o o o

Knock, knock.
Who's there?
Castor.
Castor who?
Castor oil doesn't taste good.

o o o

Knock, knock.
Who's there?
Cattle.
Cattle who?
Cattle come in if you open the door.

o o o

Knock, knock.
Who's there?
Cedar.
Cedar who?
Cedar chest is where I store my clothes.

o o o

Knock, knock.
Who's there?

Celeste.
Celeste who?
Celeste time I'm going to knock on your door.

○ ○ ○

Knock, knock.
Who's there?
Cello.
Cello who?
Cello, anybody home?

○ ○ ○

Knock, knock.
Who's there?
Censure.
Censure who?
Censure so smart, why are you telling knock-knock jokes?

○ ○ ○

Knock, knock.
Who's there?
Chair.
Chair who?
Chair your ice cream and cake with me, please.

Open the Door!

Knock, knock.
Who's there?
Charlotte.
Charlotte who?
Charlotte of people at Disneyland® today.

○ ○ ○

Knock, knock.
Who's there?
Chess.
Chess who?
Chess open the door and let me in.

○ ○ ○

Knock, knock.
Who's there?
Chester.
Chester who?
Chester minute; I'm on the telephone.

○ ○ ○

Knock, knock.
Who's there?
Chicken.
Chicken who?
Chicken to see if you are awake.

○ ○ ○

Knock, knock.
Who's there?
Ivan.
Ivan who?
Ivan to stop you from telling anymore knock-knock jokes.

○ ○ ○

Knock, knock.
Who's there?
Clothes.
Clothes who?
Clothes the window and open the door.

○ ○ ○

Knock, knock.
Who's there?
Collie.
Collie who?
Collie-fornia is where I live.

○ ○ ○

Knock, knock.
Who's there?
Comb.
Comb who?
Comb here and open the door!

○ ○ ○

Knock, knock.
Who's there?
Congo.
Congo who?
Congo to the store without money.

○ ○ ○

Knock, knock.
Who's there?
Armageddon.
Armageddon who?
Armageddon some new knock-knock jokes as soon as I can.

○ ○ ○

Knock, knock.
Who's there?
Consumption.
Consumption who?
Consumption be done to stop all these knock-knock
jokes?

○ ○ ○

Knock, knock.
Who's there?
Cumin.
Cumin who?
Cumin around the mountain when she comes.

○ ○ ○

Knock, knock.
Who's there?
Custer.
Custer who?
Custer a lot of money to buy a new car.

○ ○ ○

Knock, knock.
Who's there?
Dallas.
Dallas who?
Dallas in Wonderland.

○ ○ ○

Knock, knock.
Who's there?
Damascus.
Damascus who?
Damascus what you should wear to cover your face.

○ ○ ○

Knock, knock.
Who's there?
Darren.
Darren who?
Darren you to open the door.

○ ○ ○

Knock, knock.
Who's there?
Icon.
Icon who?
Icon hardly wait for you to open the door.

○ ○ ○

Knock, knock.
Who's there?
Despair.
Despair who?
Despair of shoes is too tight.

○ ○ ○

Knock, knock.
Who's there?
Detour.
Detour who?
Detour of the zoo starts with the monkeys.

○ ○ ○

Knock, knock.
Who's there?
Dewey.
Dewey who?
Dewey have any new knock-knock jokes?

○ ○ ○

Knock, knock.
Who's there?
Diesel.
Diesel who?
Diesel be a funny joke.

○ ○ ○

Knock, knock.
Who's there?
Frieda.
Frieda who?
Frieda going on long walks by myself.

○ ○ ○

Knock, knock.
Who's there?
Disguise.
Disguise who?
Disguise are where airplanes fly.

Who's Pounding at the Door?

Knock, knock.
Who's there?
Dismay.
Dismay who?
Dismay be my last knock-knock joke.

○ ○ ○

Knock, knock.
Who's there?
Domino.
Domino who?
Domino cowhand from the Rio Grande.

○ ○ ○

Knock, knock.
Who's there?
Dozen.
Dozen who?
Dozen anybody want to open the door?

○ ○ ○

Knock, knock.
Who's there?
Eiffel.
Eiffel who?
Eiffel good. I had a great night's sleep.

○ ○ ○

Knock, knock.
Who's there?
Eliza.
Eliza who?
Eliza lot, you can't trust him.

○ ○ ○

Knock, knock.
Who's there?
Ellen.
Ellen who?
Ellen you my bicycle if you promise to bring it back.

O O O

Knock, knock.
Who's there?
Emerson.
Emerson who?
Emerson funny knock-knock jokes.

O O O

Knock, knock.
Who's there?
Butternut.
Butternut who?
Butternut keep me standing out here in the mud.

O O O

Knock, knock.
Who's there?
Essay.
Essay who?
Essay for you to say.

O O O

Knock, knock.
Who's there?
Esther.
Esther who?
Esther anybody home?

O O O

Knock, knock.
Who's there?
E.T.
E.T. who?
E.T. too much food and you'll get fat.

○ ○ ○

Knock, knock.
Who's there?
Europe.
Europe who?
Europe early this morning, aren't you?

○ ○ ○

Knock, knock.
Who's there?
Eva.
Eva who?
Eva you let me in, I'll be happy.

○ ○ ○

Knock, knock.
Who's there?
Event.
Event who?
Event on a bicycle ride and left me alone.

○ ○ ○

Knock, knock.
Who's there?
Eyewash.
Eyewash who?
Eyewash you a happy birthday!

○ ○ ○

Knock, knock.
Who's there?
Fangs.
Fangs who?
Fangs for opening the door for me.

○ ○ ○

Knock, knock.
Who's there?
Ferry.
Ferry who?
Ferry funny. Now let me in.

○ ○ ○

Knock, knock.
Who's there?
Wren.
Wren who?
Wren you hear a new knock-knock joke, be sure to tell
me.

○ ○ ○

Knock, knock.
Who's there?
Psalm.
Psalm who?
Psalm day I'm going to get my own house.

○ ○ ○

Knock, knock.
Who's there?
Fido.
Fido who?
Fido I have to always knock at the door?

○ ○ ○

Knock, knock.
Who's there?
Venus.
Venus who?
Venus you going to stop telling knock-knock jokes?

○ ○ ○

Knock, knock.
Who's there?
Fire.
Fire who?
Fire engine has a dog with black and white spots riding it.

○ ○ ○

Knock, knock.
Who's there?
Flea.
Flea who?
Flea bit me on the arm.

Let Me In!

Knock, knock.
Who's there?
Folder.
Folder who?
Folder clothes; your room's messy.

○ ○ ○

Knock, knock.
Who's there?
Formosa.
Formosa who?
Formosa my life I have enjoyed knock-knock jokes.

○ ○ ○

Knock, knock.
Who's there?
Forty.
Forty who?
Forty crying out loud…let me in!

○ ○ ○

Knock, knock.
Who's there?
Foyer.
Foyer who?
Foyer information, I'm not going to tell you.

○ ○ ○

Knock, knock.
Who's there?
Francis.
Francis who?
Francis where they make French fries.

○ ○ ○

Knock, knock.
Who's there?
Celeste.
Celeste who?
Celeste time I'm coming to your house. You better let me in.

○ ○ ○

Knock, knock.
Who's there?
Frayda.
Frayda who?
Frayda me? Is that why you won't open the door?

○ ○ ○

Knock, knock.
Who's there?
Freddy.
Freddy who?
Freddy or not, here I come.

○ ○ ○

Knock, knock.
Who's there?
Fresno.
Fresno who?
Fresno way I'm going to stay out here!

○ ○ ○

Knock, knock.
Who's there?
Frieda.
Frieda who?
Frieda me a big pizza, please.

○ ○ ○

Knock, knock.
Who's there?
Ghana.
Ghana who?
Ghana not pout. Ghana not cry...I'm telling you why...
Santa Claus is coming to town.

○ ○ ○

Knock, knock.
Who's there?
Gibbon.
Gibbon who?
Gibbon me a break.

○ ○ ○

Knock, knock.
Who's there?
Gladys.
Gladys who?
Gladys not snowing.

○ ○ ○

Knock, knock.
Who's there?
Orange.
Orange who?
Orange you going to let me in?

○ ○ ○

Knock, knock.
Who's there?
Gopher.
Gopher who?
Gopher a walk around the block?

○ ○ ○

Knock, knock.
Who's there?
Gopher.
Gopher who?
Gopher a plane ride?

○ ○ ○

Knock, knock.
Who's there?
Gomez.
Gomez who?
Gomez around with me, buddy.

○ ○ ○

Knock, knock.
Who's there?
Kansas.
Kansas who?
Kansas what you put soda pop in.

○ ○ ○

Knock, knock.
Who's there?
Gulls.
Gulls who?
Gulls like to go shopping at the mall.

○ ○ ○

Knock, knock.
Who's there?
Habit.
Habit who?
Habit you can't guess.

○ ○ ○

Knock, knock.
Who's there?
Haddock.
Haddock who?
Haddock's killing me—got some aspirin?

○ ○ ○

Knock, knock.
Who's there?
Thistle.
Thistle who?
Thistle make you laugh.

○ ○ ○

Knock, knock.
Who's there?
Hammond.
Hammond who?
Hammond eggs for breakfast.

Stop That Noise!

Knock, knock.
Who's there?
Hank.
Hank who?
Hank E. Chief is what I blow my nose on.

○ ○ ○

Knock, knock.
Who's there?
Hannah.
Hannah who?
Hannah me a check for $1,000, please.

○ ○ ○

Knock, knock.
Who's there?
Harry.
Harry who?
Harry up and open the door.

○ ○ ○

Knock, knock.
Who's there?
Abbot.
Abbot who?
Abbot time you came to the door.

○ ○ ○

Knock, knock.
Who's there?
Dewey.
Dewey who?
Dewey have any way to stop telling knock-knock jokes?

○ ○ ○

Knock, knock.
Who's there?
Harvey.
Harvey who?
Harvey a good time yet?

○ ○ ○

Knock, knock.
Who's there?
Ali.
Ali who?
Ali, Ali oxen free.

○ ○ ○

Knock, knock.
Who's there?
Hassan.
Hassan who?
Hassan anybody heard me knocking?

○ ○ ○

Knock, knock.
Who's there?
Havana.
Havana who?
Havana go to grandmother's house for Thanksgiving.

○ ○ ○

Knock, knock.
Who's there?
Heaven.
Heaven who?
Heaven you got anything else to do?

○ ○ ○

Knock, knock.
Who's there?
Heidi.
Heidi who?
Heidi ho and away we go.

○ ○ ○

Knock, knock.
Who's there?
Henny.
Henny who?
Henny penny the sky is falling.

○ ○ ○

Knock, knock.
Who's there?
Henrietta.
Henrietta who?
Henrietta hamburger, French fries, and a milkshake.

○ ○ ○

Knock, knock.
Who's there?
Hester.
Hester who?
Hester moment and I'll tell you.

○ ○ ○

Knock, knock.
Who's there?
Hive.
Hive who?
Hive been counting my pennies.

○ ○ ○

Knock, knock.
Who's there?
Hominy.
Hominy who?
Hominy times do I have to knock?

o o o

Knock, knock.
Who's there?
Honeybee.
Honeybee who?
Honeybee nice and stop telling these knock-knock jokes.

o o o

Knock, knock.
Who's there?
Honeydew.
Honeydew who?
Honeydew you want to go on a date?

o o o

Knock, knock.
Who's there?
Hoosier.
Hoosier who?
Hoosier afraid of, the person who locked the door?

o o o

Knock, knock,
Who's there?
Hootie.
Hootie who?
Hootie think is knocking on the door?

o o o

Knock, knock.
Who's there?
Hopi.
Hopi who?
Hopi's going to open the door soon.

○ ○ ○

Knock, knock.
Who's there?
House.
House who?
House about letting me inside?

○ ○ ○

Knock, knock.
Who's there?
Howard.
Howard who?
Howard and I can keep a secret.

What's That Noise?

Knock, knock.
Who's there?
Hugh.
Hugh who?
Hugh must be sick and tired of listening to all of these
knock-knock jokes.

○ ○ ○

Knock, knock.
Who's there?
Howell.
Howell who?
Howell like to sing a solo tonight.

○ ○ ○

Knock, knock.
Who's there?
Howdy.
Howdy who?
Howdy get someone to listen to me?

○ ○ ○

Knock, knock.
Who's there?
Hugo.
Hugo who?
Hugo outside and play soccer.

○ ○ ○

Knock, knock.
Who's there?
Humus.

Humus who?
Humus be tired of listening to all these knock-knock
jokes.

○ ○ ○

Knock, knock.
Who's there?
Dinosaur.
Dinosaur who?
Dinosaur because he stubbed his toe.

○ ○ ○

Knock, knock.
Who's there?
I am.
I am who?
You mean you don't know who you are?

○ ○ ○

Knock, knock.
Who's there?
Icon.
Icon who?
Icon give you a big hug.

○ ○ ○

Knock, knock.
Who's there?
Ida.
Ida who?
Ida like to come inside.

○ ○ ○

Knock, knock.
Who's there?
Ida Mann.
Ida Mann who?
Ida Mann that you should let in.

o o o

Knock, knock.
Who's there?
Iguana.
Iguana who?
Iguana hold your hand.

o o o

Knock, knock.
Who's there?
Imus.
Imus who?
Imus be out of my mind to stay out here.

o o o

Knock, knock.
Who's there?
Lyle.
Lyle who?
Lyle be seeing you in all the old familiar places.

o o o

Knock, knock.
Who's there?
Iona.
Iona who?
Iona new car.

o o o

Knock, knock.
Who's there?
Iowa.
Iowa who?
Iowa lotta money to the I.R.S.

○ ○ ○

Knock, knock.
Who's there?
Iran.
Iran who?
Iran in a marathon.

○ ○ ○

Knock, knock.
Who's there?
Iraq.
Iraq who?
Iraq'ed up a big bill.

○ ○ ○

Knock, knock.
Who's there?
Irish.
Irish who?
Irish you a Happy New Year.

○ ○ ○

Knock, knock.
Who's there?
Isabelle.
Isabelle who?
Isabelle working on your door?

○ ○ ○

Knock, knock.
Who's there?
Israel.
Israel who?
Israel happy to see you.

ooo

Knock, knock.
Who's there?
Huron.
Huron who?
Huron my foot…please get off.

ooo

Knock, knock.
Who's there?
Ivan.
Ivan who?
Ivan to go get a hamburger.

ooo

Knock, knock.
Who's there?
Ivana.
Ivana who?
Ivana marathon race.

I'm All Knocked Out!

Knock, knock.
Who's there?
I wish.
I wish who?
I wish Setter is the name of a dog.

○ ○ ○

Knock, knock.
Who's there?
Jamaica.
Jamaica who?
Jamaica me a chocolate cake?

○ ○ ○

Knock, knock.
Who's there?
Jest.
Jest who?
Jest one of those crazy days.

○ ○ ○

Knock, knock.
Who's there?
Jester.
Jester who?
Jester 'nother knock-knock joke.

○ ○ ○

Knock, knock.
Who's there?
Jewel.
Jewel who?
Jewel never know until you open the door.

○ ○ ○

Knock, knock.
Who's there?
Saul.
Saul who?
Saul you have to do is look out the window.

○ ○ ○

Knock, knock.
Who's there?
Juan.
Juan who?
Juan day my prince will come.

○ ○ ○

Knock, knock.
Who's there?
Juicy.
Juicy who?
Juicy any one else out here?

○ ○ ○

Knock, knock.
Who's there?
Juliet.
Juliet who?
Juliet pancakes for breakfast.

○ ○ ○

Knock, knock.
Who's there?
July.
July who?
July to me and I won't tell you.

○ ○ ○

Knock, knock.
Who's there?
Juneau.
Juneau who?
Juneau anything else but knock-knock jokes?

○ ○ ○

Knock, knock.
Who's there?
Juno.
Juno who?
Juno anyone who will open the door?

○ ○ ○

Knock, knock.
Who's there?
Kansas.
Kansas who?
Kansas be the way to get in?

○ ○ ○

Knock, knock.
Who's there?
Kareem.
Kareem who?
Kareem of wheat is good to eat.

○ ○ ○

Knock, knock.
Who's there?
Ken.
Ken who?
Ken you stop telling these knock-knock jokes?

○ ○ ○

Knock, knock.
Who's there?
Kent.
Kent who?
Kent you see?

o o o

Knock, knock.
Who's there?
Kenya.
Kenya who?
Kenya get me a drink? I'm thirsty.

o o o

Knock, knock.
Who's there?
Ketchup.
Ketchup who?
Ketchup on all the gossip.

o o o

Knock, knock.
Who's there?
Kleenex.
Kleenex who?
Kleenex happen after you take a bath.

o o o

Knock, knock.
Who's there?
Kuwait.
Kuwait who?
Kuwait till I tie my shoe.

o o o

Knock, knock.
Who's there?
Lego.
Lego who?
Lego of the door handle.

○ ○ ○

Knock, knock.
Who's there?
Leif.
Leif who?
Leifs are what grow on trees.

○ ○ ○

Knock, knock.
Who's there?
Lena.
Lena who?
Lena against the door and you'll fall over when I open it.

Knock It Off!

Knock, knock.
Who's there?
Lenny.
Lenny who?
Lenny body home?

○ ○ ○

Knock, knock.
Who's there?
Leon.
Leon who?
Leon me when you get tired.

○ ○ ○

Knock, knock.
Who's there?
Les.
Les who?
Les get your doorbell fixed.

○ ○ ○

Knock, knock.
Who's there?
Lettie.
Lettie who?
Lettie the dog out so I can play with him.

○ ○ ○

Knock, knock.
Who's there?
Lettuce.
Lettuce who?
Lettuce tell another knock-knock joke.

○ ○ ○

Knock, knock.
Who's there?
Lewis.
Lewis who?
Lewis always a good friend to me.

○ ○ ○

Knock, knock.
Who's there?
License.
License who?
He didn't license the last time.

○ ○ ○

Knock, knock.
Who's there?
Lima bean.
Lima bean who?
Lima bean playing in the mud.

○ ○ ○

Knock, knock.
Who's there?
Lion.
Lion who?
Lion down on the beach for a suntan.

○ ○ ○

Knock, knock.
Who's there?
Lionel.
Lionel who?
Lionel eat you if you come too close.

○ ○ ○

Knock, knock.
Who's there?
Lisa.
Lisa who?
Lisa new motorcycle for $200.

○ ○ ○

Knock, knock.
Who's there?
Liver.
Liver who?
To be a liver is better than being a dier.

○ ○ ○

Knock, knock.
Who's there?
Llama.
Llama who?
Llama so glad you like knock-knock jokes.

○ ○ ○

Knock, knock.
Who's there?
Locker.
Locker who?
Un locker the door and let me in.

○ ○ ○

Knock, knock.
Who's there?
Lois.
Lois who?
Lois man on the totem pole.

○ ○ ○

Knock, knock.
Who's there?
Loren.
Loren who?
Loren order's what you need in a courtroom?

○ ○ ○

Knock, knock.
Who's there?
Lorraine.
Lorraine who?
Lorraine keeps coming and I can't play outside.

○ ○ ○

Knock, knock.
Who's there?
Louisville.
Louisville who?
Louisville you please tell me another knock-knock joke?

○ ○ ○

Knock, knock.
Who's there?
Luke.
Luke who?
Luke out the window and see.

○ ○ ○

Knock, knock.
Who's there?
Lyle.
Lyle who?
Lyle get you into trouble.

○ ○ ○

Knock, knock.
Who's there?
Madison.
Madison who?
Madison is what doctors give you when you are sick.

○ ○ ○

Knock, knock.
Who's there?
Major.
Major who?
Major ask, didn't I?

○ ○ ○

Knock, knock.
Who's there?
Mary Hannah.
Mary Hannah who?
Mary Hannah little lamb; its fleece was white as snow.

Who's Beating the Door Down?

Knock, knock.
Who's there?
Mary Lee.
Mary Lee who?
Mary Lee Christmas.

○ ○ ○

Knock, knock.
Who's there?
Maura.
Maura who?
Maura knock-knock jokes drives me crazy.

○ ○ ○

Knock, knock.
Who's there?
Maya.
Maya who?
Maya bicycle is broken.

○ ○ ○

Knock, knock.
Who's there?
Mega.
Mega who?
Mega me an apple pie.

○ ○ ○

Knock, knock.
Who's there?
Megan.
Megan who?
Megan a funny joke is what I like to do.

○ ○ ○

Knock, knock.
Who's there?
Melrose.
Melrose who?
Melrose up early in the morning.

○ ○ ○

Knock, knock.
Who's there?
Miners.
Miners who?
Miners the biggest piece of cake.

○ ○ ○

Knock, knock.
Who's there?
Minnie.
Minnie who?
Minnie laughs to you.

○ ○ ○

Knock, knock.
Who's there?
Mister.
Mister who?
Mister bus to school.

○ ○ ○

Knock, knock.
Who's there?
Mummy.
Mummy who?
Mummy's what it takes to buy a car.

○ ○ ○

Knock, knock.
Who's there?
Hugh.
Hugh who?
Hugh are really great at telling knock-knock jokes.

○ ○ ○

Knock, knock.
Who's there?
Musket.
Musket who?
Musket a new joke book.

○ ○ ○

Knock, knock.
Who's there?
Myth.
Myth who?
Myth me? I myth you.

○ ○ ○

Knock, knock.
Who's there?
Nero.
Nero who?
Nero the door, so let me in.

○ ○ ○

Knock, knock.
Who's there?
Owen.
Owen who?
Owen are you ever going to open the door?

○ ○ ○

Knock, knock.
Who's there?
Newton.
Newton who?
Newton had an apple fall on his head.

o o o

Knock, knock.
Who's there?
Niacin.
Niacin who?
Niacin quiet around here.

o o o

Knock, knock.
Who's there?
Noah.
Noah who?
Noah good knock-knock joke?

o o o

Knock, knock.
Who's there?
Noah.
Noah who?
Noah anybody who will open the door?

o o o

Knock, knock.
Who's there?
Norway.
Norway who?
Norway am I going to stand outside.

o o o

Knock, knock.
Who's there?
Noun.
Noun who?
Noun the time to open the door.

○ ○ ○

Knock, knock.
Who's there?
Nuisance.
Nuisance who?
What's the nuisance of telling any more knock-knock jokes?

Hold Your Horses!

Knock, knock.
Who's there?
Odessa.
Odessa who?
Odessa funny joke.

○ ○ ○

Knock, knock.
Who's there?
Ohio.
Ohio who?
Ohio can you jump?

○ ○ ○

Knock, knock.
Who's there?
Oil.
Oil who?
Oil the hinges of the door.

○ ○ ○

Knock, knock.
Who's there?
Oink, Oink.
Oink, Oink who?
Are you part pig?
No, part owl.

○ ○ ○

Knock, knock.
Who's there?
Olga.
Olga who?
Olga play with my friends.

○ ○ ○

Knock, knock.
Who's there?
Olive.
Olive who?
Olive on the other side of the street.

○ ○ ○

Knock, knock.
Who's there?
Oliver.
Oliver who?
Oliver town people are laughing at knock-knock jokes.

○ ○ ○

Knock, knock.
Who's there?
Oman.
Oman who?
Oman! Is it cold out here!

○ ○ ○

Knock, knock.
Who's there?
Omelet.
Omelet who?
Omelet happier reading this book.

○ ○ ○

Knock, knock.
Who's there?
Omen.
Omen who?
Omen, do I want to come inside!

○ ○ ○

Knock, knock.
Who's there?
Clare.
Clare who?
Clare out of the way! I'm comin' in!

○ ○ ○

Knock, knock.
Who's there?
Orange.
Orange who?
Orange you going to tell me another knock-knock joke?

○ ○ ○

Knock, knock.
Who's there?
Otter.
Otter who?
Otter in the court!

○ ○ ○

Knock, knock.
Who's there?
Osborne.
Osborne who?
Osborne in California.

○ ○ ○

Knock, knock.
Who's there?
Emma.
Emma who?
Emma laughing at all of these knock-knock jokes.

○ ○ ○

Knock, knock.
Who's there?
Oscar.
Oscar who?
Oscar if she wants to come out and play.

○ ○ ○

Knock, knock.
Who's there?
Ostrich.
Ostrich who?
Ostrich when I get up in the morning.

○ ○ ○

Knock, knock.
Who's there?
Otis.
Otis who?
Otis is a funny joke.

○ ○ ○

Knock, knock.
Who's there?
Ida.
Ida who?
Ida wanna hear any more knock-knock jokes.

○ ○ ○

Knock, knock.
Who's there?
Otto.
Otto who?
Otto let me in.

○ ○ ○

Knock, knock.
Who's there?
Owen.
Owen who?
Owen can I get my allowance?

○ ○ ○

Knock, knock.
Who's there?
Owl.
Owl who?
Owl be seeing you later.

○ ○ ○

Knock, knock.
Who's there?
Garter.
Garter who?
Garter snakes crawl on the ground.

Tap, Tap, Tap!

Knock, knock.
Who's there?
Owl go.
Owl go who?
Of course owl go who.

○ ○ ○

Knock, knock.
Who's there?
Ozzie.
Ozzie who?
Ozzie you later, alligator.

○ ○ ○

Knock, knock.
Who's there?
Pasta.
Pasta who?
Pasta peanut butter sandwich.

○ ○ ○

Knock, knock.
Who's there?
Pear.
Pear who?
Pear-haps you will stop telling silly jokes.

○ ○ ○

Knock, knock.
Who's there?
Shoes.
Shoes who?
Shoes me, but I've heard this joke before.

○ ○ ○

Knock, knock.
Who's there?
Pecan.
Pecan who?
Pecan someone your own size.

○ ○ ○

Knock, knock.
Who's there?
Pencil.
Pencil who?
Pencil fall if you lose too much weight.

○ ○ ○

Knock, knock.
Who's there?
Pepper.
Pepper who?
Pepper up and make her open the door!

○ ○ ○

Knock, knock.
Who's there?
Pest.
Pest who?
Pest the dessert, please.

○ ○ ○

Knock, knock.
Who's there?
Phillip.
Phillip who?
Phillip your piggy bank with money.

○ ○ ○

Knock, knock.
Who's there?
Phyllis.
Phyllis who?
Phyllis in on the latest joke.

○ ○ ○

Knock, knock.
Who's there?
Pig.
Pig who?
Pig up your room; it's a mess.

○ ○ ○

Knock, knock.
Who's there?
Pizza.
Pizza who?
Pizza cake would taste good.

○ ○ ○

Knock, knock.
Who's there?
Saul.
Saul who?
Saul these jokes are too much for me.

○ ○ ○

Knock, knock.
Who's there?
Police.
Police who?
Police let me in.

○ ○ ○

Knock, knock.
Who's there?
Irish stew.
Irish stew who?
Irish stew would stop telling all these knock-knock jokes.

o o o

Knock, knock.
Who's there?
Police.
Police who?
Police give me a candy bar.

o o o

Knock, knock.
Who's there?
Police.
Police who?
Police give me a break.

o o o

Knock, knock.
Who's there?
Pollyanna.
Pollyanna who?
Pollyanna cracker.

o o o

Knock, knock.
Who's there?
Polyp.
Polyp who?
Polyp a chair and sit down.

○ ○ ○

Knock, knock.
Who's there?
Psalm.
Psalm who?
Psalm can't stand knock-knock jokes.

○ ○ ○

Knock, knock.
Who's there?
Quiche.
Quiche who?
Quiche me and I'll quiche you.

○ ○ ○

Knock, knock.
Who's there?
Lennie.
Lennie who?
Lennie me your surfboard.

Stop Beating the Door!

Knock, knock.
Who's there?
Queen.
Queen who?
Queen the dirty dishes.

○ ○ ○

Knock, knock.
Who's there?
Racine.
Racine who?
Racine around in circles.

○ ○ ○

Knock, knock.
Who's there?
Wendy.
Wendy who?
Wendy weather blows leaves.

○ ○ ○

Knock, knock.
Who's there?
Raisin.
Raisin who?
Raisin kids is not easy.

○ ○ ○

Knock, knock.
Who's there?
Rapture.
Rapture who?
Rapture presents for Christmas.

○ ○ ○

Knock, knock.
Who's there?
Ray.
Ray who?
Ray who is a dyslexic cheerleader.

○ ○ ○

Knock, knock.
Who's there?
Razor.
Razor who?
Razor window and talk with me.

○ ○ ○

Knock, knock.
Who's there?
Delight.
Delight who?
Delight on the candle burnt my finger.

○ ○ ○

Knock, knock.
Who's there?
Rhino.
Rhino who?
Rhino something you don't.

○ ○ ○

Knock, knock.
Who's there?
Rhoda.
Rhoda who?
Rhoda 'round the block a few times.

○ ○ ○

Knock, knock.
Who's there?
Rice.
Rice who?
Rice up early in the morning.

○ ○ ○

Knock, knock.
Who's there?
Roach.
Roach who?
Roach you a Valentine card.

○ ○ ○

Knock, knock.
Who's there?
Rocco.
Rocco who?
Rocco roll is my favorite kind of music.

○ ○ ○

Knock, knock.
Who's there?
Roland.
Roland who?
Roland down the river.

○ ○ ○

Knock, knock.
Who's there?
Jamaica.
Jamaica who?
Jamaica up a new knock-knock joke?

○ ○ ○

Knock, knock.
Who's there?
Russia.
Russia who?
Russia around because I'm late.

○ ○ ○

Knock, knock.
Who's there?
Saber.
Saber who?
Saber—she's drowning!

○ ○ ○

Knock, knock.
Who's there?
Eiffel.
Eiffel who?
Eiffel down and skinned my knee.

○ ○ ○

Knock, knock.
Who's there?
Freddy.
Freddy who?
Freddy cat, Freddy cat.

○ ○ ○

Knock, knock.
Who's there?
Sam.
Sam who?
Sam person who's been standing outside.

○ ○ ○

Knock, knock.
Who's there?
Sanitize.
Sanitize who?
Sanitize his shoes before he brings presents.

○ ○ ○

Knock, knock.
Who's there?
Sarah.
Sarah who?
Sarah some way to get you to open the door?

○ ○ ○

Knock, knock.
Who's there?
Duet.
Duet who?
Duet dinner already?

What's That Rapping Noise?

Knock, knock.
Who's there?
Sasha.
Sasha who?
Sasha fuss over trying to get into the house!

○ ○ ○

Knock, knock.
Who's there?
Doris.
Doris who?
Doris always closed…do you ever open it?

○ ○ ○

Knock, knock.
Who's there?
Sawyer.
Sawyer who?
Sawyer picture on a wanted poster.

○ ○ ○

Knock, knock.
Who's there?
Scold.
Scold who?
Scold out here…let me in.

○ ○ ○

Knock, knock.
Who's there?
Scott.
Scott who?
Scott a lot more of these jokes.

○ ○ ○

Scratch, scratch.
Who's there?
I'm too weak to knock; the cat wants in.

○ ○ ○

Knock, knock.
Who's there?
Séance.
Séance who?
Séance you won't open the door, I'm going to leave.

○ ○ ○

Knock, knock.
Who's there?
Senior.
Senior who?
Senior picture in the funny pages.

○ ○ ○

Knock, knock.
Who's there?
Seymour.
Seymour who?
Seymour bad weather coming.

○ ○ ○

Knock, knock.
Who's there?
Sheik.
Sheik who?
Sheik around the house and find the door key.

○ ○ ○

Knock, knock.
Who's there?

Shelby.
Shelby who?
Shelby taking her horse for a ride.

o o o

Knock, knock.
Who's there?
Sherwood.
Sherwood who?
Sherwood like to hear some more jokes.

o o o

Knock, knock.
Who's there?
Shirley.
Shirley who?
Shirley this isn't your last knock-knock joke.

o o o

Knock, knock.
Who's there?
Shoe.
Shoe who?
Shoe me a good time.

o o o

Knock, knock.
Who's there?
Shore.
Shore who?
Shore am tired of knocking.

o o o

Knock, knock.
Who's there?

Sid.
Sid who?
Sid down and tell me a story.

○ ○ ○

Knock, knock.
Who's there?
Skit.
Skit who?
Skit down and watch the football game.

○ ○ ○

Knock, knock.
Who's there?
Snake.
Snake who?
Snake hands…it's nice to meet you.

○ ○ ○

Knock, knock.
Who's there?
Soda.
Soda who?
Soda you want to let me in or not?

○ ○ ○

Knock, knock.
Who's there?
Sole.
Sole who?
Sole on my shoe; it has a hole in it.

○ ○ ○

Knock, knock.
Who's there?

Solo.
Solo who?
Solo I can't see you.

○ ○ ○

Knock, knock.
Who's there?
Sony.
Sony who?
Sony day, isn't it?

○ ○ ○

Knock, knock.
Who's there?
Spin.
Spin who?
Spin too long—now open the door.

The Doorbell Is Broken!

Knock, knock.
Who's there?
Stefan.
Stefan who?
It's Stefanitly a funny joke.

○ ○ ○

Knock, knock.
Who's there?
Stella.
Stella who?
Stella want to come in.

○ ○ ○

Knock, knock.
Who's there?
Stu.
Stu who?
Stu you ever get tired of all these knock-knock jokes?

○ ○ ○

Knock, knock.
Who's there?
Succumb.
Succumb who?
Succumb outside and see who it is.

○ ○ ○

Knock, knock.
Who's there?
Sue.
Sue who?
Sue who do you think it is?

○ ○ ○

Knock, knock.
Who's there?
Suede.
Suede who?
Suede down upon the Swanee River.

○ ○ ○

Knock, knock.
Who's there?
Summer.
Summer who?
Summer better than others at telling knock-knock jokes.

○ ○ ○

Knock, knock.
Who's there?
Summer.
Summer who?
Summer my friends like knock-knock jokes.

○ ○ ○

Knock, knock.
Who's there?
Surly.
Surly who?
Surly to bed and surly to rise makes a man healthy,
wealthy, and wise.

○ ○ ○

Knock, knock.
Who's there?
Suture.
Suture who?
Suture funny joke.

○ ○ ○

Knock, knock.
Who's there?
Swarm.
Swarm who?
Swarm weather is better than cold weather.

○ ○ ○

Knock, knock.
Who's there?
Swatter.
Swatter who?
Swatter's getting down my neck. Let me in!

○ ○ ○

Knock, knock.
Who's there?
Switch.
Switch who?
Switch on the light and see.

○ ○ ○

Knock, knock.
Who's there?
Taiwan.
Taiwan who?
Taiwan hear another knock-knock joke?

○ ○ ○

Knock, knock.
Who's there?
Tally.
Tally who?
Are you from England?

○ ○ ○

Knock, knock.
Who's there?
Tanks.
Tanks who?
Tanks for opening the door.

○ ○ ○

Knock, knock.
Who's there?
Tennis.
Tennis who?
Tennis just before eleven.

○ ○ ○

Knock, knock.
Who's there?
Juneau.
Juneau who?
Juneau any more knock-knock jokes?

○ ○ ○

Knock, knock.
Who's there?
Ants are.
Ants are who?
Ants are the door, please.

○ ○ ○

Knock, knock.
Who's there?
Thermos.
Thermos who?
Thermos be some way to get you to open the door.

○ ○ ○

Knock, knock.
Who's there?
Thesis.
Thesis who?
Thesis almost the end of the book.

○ ○ ○

Knock, knock.
Who's there?
Jimmy.
Jimmy who?
Jimmy your key so I can open the door.

Please Go Away!

Knock, knock.
Who's there?
Think?
Think who?
You're welcome!

○ ○ ○

Knock, knock.
Who's there?
Thor.
Thor who?
I'm Thor from stubbing my big toe.

○ ○ ○

Knock, knock.
Who's there?
Thumb.
Thumb who?
Thumb day my prince will come.

○ ○ ○

Knock, knock.
Who's there?
Dishes.
Dishes who?
Dishes another great joke.

○ ○ ○

Knock, knock.
Who's there?
Tibet.
Tibet who?
You know, Tibet way to get in is to use your key.

○ ○ ○

Knock, knock.
Who's there?
Tijuana.
Tijuana who?
Tijuana hold my hand?

○ ○ ○

Knock, knock.
Who's there?
Tire.
Tire who?
Tire your shoestrings before you trip and fall.

○ ○ ○

Knock, knock.
Who's there?
Tree.
Tree who?
Tree more days till Christmas.

○ ○ ○

Knock, knock.
Who's there?
Stella.
Stella who?
Stella out here knocking.

○ ○ ○

Knock, knock.
Who's there?
Tulsa.
Tulsa who?
Please Tulsa 'nother knock-knock joke.

○ ○ ○

Knock, knock.
Who's there?
Turner.
Turner who?
Turner the pancakes before they burn.

○ ○ ○

Knock, knock.
Who's there?
Turnip.
Turnip who?
Turnip the television, I can't hear it.

○ ○ ○

Knock, knock.
Who's there?
Twain.
Twain who?
Twain yourself for a big race.

○ ○ ○

Knock, knock.
Who's there?
Oscar.
Oscar who?
Oscar to open the door.

○ ○ ○

Knock, knock.
Who's there?
Unaware.
Unaware who?
Unaware is what you wear under your clothes.

○ ○ ○

Knock, knock.
Who's there?
Uneeda.
Uneeda who?
Uneeda brush your teeth.

○ ○ ○

Knock, knock.
Who's there?
Harris.
Harris who?
Harris nice, especially if you are bald.

○ ○ ○

Knock, knock.
Who's there?
Upton.
Upton who?
Upton you to open the door.

○ ○ ○

Knock, knock.
Who's there?
Van Nuys.
Van Nuys who?
Van Nuys have seen the glory...

○ ○ ○

Knock, knock.
Who's there?
Water.
Water who?
Water the matter with you?

○ ○ ○

Knock, knock.
Who's there?
Veal.
Veal who?
Veal see you later.

o o o

Knock, knock.
Who's there?
Venice.
Venice who?
Venice you going to open the door?

o o o

Knock, knock.
Who's there?
Venue.
Venue who?
Venue stop telling knock-knock jokes, I'll be glad.

Stop That Pounding!

Knock, knock.
Who's there?
Vera.
Vera who?
Vera tired of knock-knock jokes.

○ ○ ○

Knock, knock.
Who's there?
Vine.
Vine who?
Vine weather to go swimming.

○ ○ ○

Knock, knock.
Who's there?
Viper.
Viper who?
Viper feet, your shoes are muddy.

○ ○ ○

Knock, knock.
Who's there?
Ven.
Ven who?
Ven will you finally stop telling knock-knock jokes?

○ ○ ○

Knock, knock.
Who's there?
Vance.
Vance who?
Vance in a while we come up with a new knock-knock
joke.

○ ○ ○

Knock, knock.
Who's there?
Wa.
Wa who?
Hey, are you a cowboy?

○ ○ ○

Knock, knock.
Who's there?
Wade.
Wade who?
Wade in the water and get wet.

○ ○ ○

Knock, knock.
Who's there?
Wanda.
Wanda who?
Wanda hold my hand?

○ ○ ○

Knock, knock.
Who's there?
Warner.
Warner who?
Warner hear another knock-knock joke?

○ ○ ○

Knock, knock.
Who's there?
Warrior.
Warrior who?
Warrior been all of my life?

O O O

Knock, knock.
Who's there?
Weed.
Weed who?
Weed better stop telling these knock-knock jokes.

O O O

Knock, knock.
Who's there?
Weird.
Weird who?
Weird you hear that joke?

O O O

Knock, knock.
Who's there?
Wendell.
Wendell who?
Wendell you let me in?

O O O

Knock, knock.
Who's there?
Wendy.
Wendy who?
Wendy red, red robin comes bob, bob bobbin' along.

O O O

Knock, knock.
Who's there?
Wet.
Wet who?
Wet me tell you a funny story.

○ ○ ○

Knock, knock.
Who's there?
Winnie.
Winnie who?
Winnie funnier joke comes along, we'll tell it.

○ ○ ○

Knock, knock.
Who's there?
Wooden shoe.
Wooden shoe who?
Wooden shoe like to hear another joke?

○ ○ ○

Knock, knock.
Who's there?
Xavier.
Xavier who?
Xavier breath.

○ ○ ○

Knock, knock.
Who's there?
Zany.
Zany who?
Zany body home?

○ ○ ○

Knock, knock.
Who's there?
Zinging.
Zinging who?
Zinging a song.

○ ○ ○

Knock, knock.
Who's there?
Police.
Police who?
Police open up the door.

○ ○ ○

Knock, knock.
Who's there?
Mister.
Mister who?
Mister at my birthday party.

You Have the Wrong Address!

Knock, knock.
Who's there?
Micky.
Micky who?
Micky won't work in the door lock.

○ ○ ○

Knock, knock.
Who's there?
Cereal.
Cereal who?
Cereal nice of you to open the door.

○ ○ ○

Knock, knock.
Who's there?
Alec.
Alec who?
Alec my ice-cream cone.

○ ○ ○

Knock, knock.
Who's there?
Colin.
Colin who?
Colin you on the telephone.

○ ○ ○

Knock, knock.
Who's there?
Sid.
Sid who?
Sid down and rest awhile.

○ ○ ○

Knock, knock.
Who's there?
Teresa.
Teresa who?
Teresa green and the sky is blue.

o o o

Knock, knock.
Who's there?
Noah.
Noah who?
Noah more knock-knock jokes if you let me in.

o o o

Knock, knock.
Who's there?
Justin.
Justin who?
Justin time to open the door, it's cold outside.

o o o

Knock, knock.
Who's there?
Ken.
Ken who?
Ken you come out and play?

o o o

Knock, knock.
Who's there?
Howard.
Howard who?
Howard you like to be outside in the cold?

o o o

Knock, knock.
Who's there?
Isaac.
Isaac who?
Isaac coming in as soon as you open the door.

○ ○ ○

Knock, knock.
Who's there?
Wilma.
Wilma who?
Wilma chocolate chip cookies be ready soon?

○ ○ ○

Knock, knock.
Who's there?
Ammonia.
Ammonia who?
Ammonia been out here for an hour.

○ ○ ○

Knock, knock.
Who's there?
Tennis.
Tennis who?
Tennis seven plus three.

○ ○ ○

Knock, knock.
Who's there?
Cash.
Cash who?
I thought you were nuts.

○ ○ ○

Knock, knock.
Who's there?
Arthur.
Arthur who?
Arthur any good television programs on?

o o o

Knock, knock.
Who's there?
Cynthia.
Cynthia who?
Cynthia been away, I've missed you.

o o o

Knock, knock.
Who's there?
Viola.
Viola who?
Viola sudden you don't know me?

o o o

Knock, knock.
Who's there?
Irma.
Irma who?
Irma going to keep knocking until you let me in.

o o o

Knock, knock.
Who's there?
William.
William who?
William mind bringing me an ice-cream cone?

o o o

Knock, knock.
Who's there?
Weirdo.
Weirdo who?
Weirdo you think you're going?

o o o

Knock, knock.
Who's there?
Handsome.
Handsome who?
Handsome money to me and I'll tell you.

Who Is It?

Knock, knock.
Who's there?
Nana.
Nana who?
Nana your business.

○ ○ ○

Knock, knock.
Who's there?
Yvonne.
Yvonne who?
Yvonne to go on a date?

○ ○ ○

Knock, knock.
Who's there?
Alison.
Alison who?
Alison to my CD player.

○ ○ ○

Knock, knock.
Who's there?
Irish stew.
Irish stew who?
Irish stew for speeding down the highway.

○ ○ ○

Knock, knock.
Who's there?
Lena.
Lena who?
Lena your head out the window and see.

○ ○ ○

Knock, knock.
Who's there?
Cows.
Cows who?
No, no. Cows go moo.

○ ○ ○

Knock, knock.
Who's there?
Europe.
Europe who?
Europe out of bed for a change.

○ ○ ○

Knock, knock.
Who's there?
A little old lady.
A little old lady who?
I didn't know you could yodel.

○ ○ ○

Knock, knock.
Who's there?
Lionel.
Lionel who?
Lionel get you into trouble.

○ ○ ○

Knock, knock.
Who's there?
Jester.
Jester who?
Jester minute, I'm going to cry if you don't open the door.

○ ○ ○

Knock, knock.
Who's there?
Snow.
Snow who?
Snow use guessing. Open the door and see.

o o o

Knock, knock.
Who's there?
Eva.
Eva who?
Eva you're deaf or your doorbell isn't working.

o o o

Knock, knock.
Who's there?
Oscar.
Oscar who?
Oscar silly question, get a silly answer.

o o o

Knock, knock.
Who's there?
Francis.
Francis who?
Francis in Europe.

o o o

Knock, knock.
Who's there?
Jamaica.
Jamaica who?
Jamaica me an apple pie?

o o o

Knock, knock.
Who's there?
Leaf.
Leaf who?
Leaf me outside and I'll cry.

○ ○ ○

Knock, knock.
Who's there?
Warrior.
Warrior who?
Warrior been? I've been outside for a long time.

○ ○ ○

Knock, knock.
Who's there?
Midas.
Midas who?
Midas well let me in or I'll keep knocking.

○ ○ ○

Knock, knock.
Who's there?
Theodore.
Theodore who?
Theodore is locked. Please let me in.

○ ○ ○

Knock, knock.
Who's there?
Gladys.
Gladys who?
Gladys not raining.

○ ○ ○

Knock, knock.
Who's there?
Robin.
Robin who?
Stick'em up! I'm Robin you.

o o o

Knock, knock.
Who's there?
Stu.
Stu who?
Stu you always ask questions like that?

Other Books by Bob Phillips